Dart Scripting Made Stupid Simple

Authored By

Jordan Kaufman
&
Fawzia Begum

DEDICATION

To my daughter Abigail:

do(you.age++)**while** you.age<8;
if you.age == 8
{you.knowledge+=me.knowledge.code;}

(sorry doesn't compile in Dart)

CONTENTS

FREE GIFT – Dart Code in COLOR

The Code Used in This Volume IN COLOR

Courtesy of our friend Derek Banas (from *New Think Tank*) we are happy to send you a PDF of the code from this volume.

It is even more awesome than it sounds... but in addition this will put you on our exclusive list of **Made Stupid Simple** fans and we will let you know about future titles in the **Made Stupid Simple** Series.

Get your free copy at:

http://sixfigureteen.com/dart

Dart Scripting Made Stupid Simple

About This Manual

This manual gives you a **step-by-step** programming lesson in Dart. This tutorial is designed for all those who are looking for a starting point to learn Dart.

The topics are suitable for both **beginners** as well as advanced users (although is focused on the needs of beginners). This book tells you what's cool about Dart and how to write-and-run your first Dart app and beyond. We HIGHLY recommend that you download the code examples used in this book at:

http://sixfigureteen.com/dart

Dart Programming

Dart is an **open-source**, new programming language developed by **Google**, and is used for building web, server and mobile apps. Dart is a **class-based**, single-inheritance, object-oriented language with **C-style syntax** that supports abstract classes, interfaces, reified generics, and **optional typing**.

It is not only a **new programming language**, but an editor, virtual machine (VM), libraries, and a browser that can run Dart apps natively. It is also a **compiler to JavaScript**. Keeping user demand in mind, Dart helps build the high-performance, modern apps in a more productive way.

Install Dart

Before you can start programming in Dart, you need to install the program. You also need to install Sublime Text 3 on Windows as well, and I'm here to teach you all that. So let's get started.

Windows Installation

If you are on Windows, this is how you are going to install Dart as well as make it work with Sublime Text 3. The first thing you're going to do is go to your command prompt.

Command **Prompt > RIGHT CLICK >Click > "RUN AS ADMINISTRATOR"**

Then we are going to use a really nice tool called Chocolatey. Go to:

https://chocolatey.org

With your command prompt already opened up. Then scroll down, highlight and copy the script text below:

```
c:\> @powershell -NoProfile -ExecutionPolicy Bypass -Command "iex ((new-object net.webclient).DownloadString
('https://chocolatey.org/install.ps1'))" && SET PATH=%PATH%;%
ALLUSERSPROFILE%\chocolatey\bin
```

```
PS:\>iex ((new-object net.webclient).DownloadString
('https://chocolatey.org/install.ps1'))
```

We are going to paste this text into our command prompt and run it, or hit **Enter**. Now, we should be able to use Chocolatey. You may need to restart your command prompt if you have any problems.

Next, type in the text below, ending with whatever the latest version of the program is:

```
choco install dart-sdk -version 1.11.0
```

Then you are going to hit **Enter**. That is going to run all of that script. Then it will say you need to verify that, so we are going to type in 1 and hit **Enter** again. You should get this message:

The install of dart-sdk was successful.

Now we are going to type in:

```
choco install Dartium -version 1.11.0
```

This will install a tool that we aren't actually going to use in this part of the tutorial, but it might be beneficial to you later on in your Dart development. So we might as well install it now.

Once again, it is going to ask you to verify you to Type in 1, hit **Enter**, and it will install for you as well.

Now you are all done with the command prompt and **Chocolatey**. Now let's make this work with **Sublime Text 3**. In your browser got to:

https://packagecontrol.io/installation

This is going to make it very easy for us to install things in Sublime Text 3. If you're using Sublime Text 2, go ahead and click on the Sublime Text 2 tab, and copy all of this below:

SUBLIME TEXT 3   **SUBLIME TEXT 2**

```
import urllib.request,os,hashlib; h =
'eb2297e1a458f27d836c04bb0cbaf282' +
'd0e7a3098092775ccb37ca9d6b2e4b7d'; pf = 'Package Control.sublime-
package'; ipp = sublime.installed_packages_path();
urllib.request.install_opener( urllib.request.build_opener
( urllib.request.ProxyHandler()) ); by = urllib.request.urlopen
( 'http://packagecontrol.io/' + pf.replace(' ', '%20')).read(); dh
= hashlib.sha256(by).hexdigest(); print('Error validating download
(got %s instead of %s), please try manual install' % (dh, h)) if
dh != h else open(os.path.join( ipp, pf), 'wb' ).write(by)
```

Open up Sublime Text 3 and if you don't have the console open, go to **View** and click on **Show Console**. Then you're going to paste what you got from the website down in the console below and hit **Enter**. This will allow you to use package control, which is very useful.

Once again, you may need to restart Sublime Text 3 to make this work. Now to bring it up, we are going to click on **Tools** and command palette and then type in **Install** and click on **Install Package**.

After you do that, you are going to type in **Dart** and click on **Dart** and there you go! We got a lot of things done!

It will ask you to create a path to your Dart-sdk in the **Preferences** sublime-settings.

To create the path, go to **Preferences** and click on **Settings-User**, and type:

```
{
"font_size": 15,
"Dart_sdk_path": "C:\\tools\\Dart-sdk",
"ignored_packages":
  [
     "Vintage"
  ]
}
```

Make sure you use two back slashes and then save it.

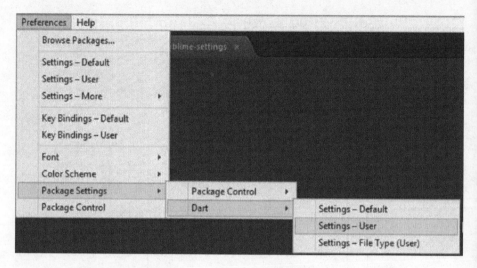

After you do that, go to:

Preferences → Package Settings → Dart → Settings-User, and type:

```
{"Dart_sdk_path":\\tools\\Dart-sdk"}
```

and save it once again.

After you have all that set up, inside your project folder wherever you will be creating all your Dart files, you need to create a file called **pupspec.yaml**.

Enter the following information:

```
name: my_project
version: 0.0.1
description: My project.
Dependencies:
path: any
```

Then click on save once more.

We want to save our project. So click on **Project** in Sublime Text 3, and go to **Save Project As**, and give your project a name. I just called it **Darttut.sublime-project**. You have to have .sublime-project, but you can call it whatever you want. After that, save the project.

Whenever you are you building everything you're going to want to click on **Tools**, go to **Build System**, and to **Dart-pubspec**, and make sure that this is check marked.

Then you're going to verify it again within the same folder wherever you have **pubspec.yaml,** and where you saved your project. In there, you want to create a new file and make sure the **.dart** extension goes with your filename.

Then Type:

```
Void main() {
      print("Hello, worlds"); }
```

To verify that everything is working for us, hit **F7** or **Shift F7** to run and as you can see that everything is (or at least should be) running fine.

Mac Installation

Now let's get on with installing Dart for you Mac Users (if you happen to be one of *those mac people* that enjoys the cozy and costly confines of the apple world).

What I have below is an HTML file. I just called it **Darttut.html** and created everything you see below. I also went ahead and put the styling inside, so we would have everything in one file, and that will save some time as well.

darttut.html

```
1   <!DOCTYPE html>
2   <html>
3   <style>
4   body {font-size: 2em;}
5   input[type="text"]{font-size: .9em;}
6   input[type=submit] {
7       border: 2px solid black; background: #E5E4E2;
8       font-size: .5em; font-weight: bold; color: black;
9       padding: .8em 2em;
10      margin-top: .4em;
11  }
12  #output {font-size: .9em; margin-top: .4em;}
13  .titleStyle {font-size: 2.3em;}
14  </style>
15    <body>
16      <span id ="sum">Calculation</span><br>
17      <input type ="text" id ="num1"><br>
18      <input type ="text" id ="num2"><br>
19      <input type ="submit" value ="Add" id ="button">
20      <br>
21      <textarea rows="20" cols="50" id="output">Program Output</textarea>
22      <div id="divBox"></div>
23
24      <script type="application/dart" src="darttut.dart">
25      </script>
26
27      <script src="darttut.js"></script>
28
29    </body>
30  </html>
```

What we are basically going to be doing is targeting the IDs.

The first line on the right will be **num1,** the second line will be **num2,** and the **Add** button on the right will have the ID of the button.

What we are going to need to do is, bring in the script for our Dart file or our JavaScript, which is what our Dart file is going to be created into, or converted into. If you want to import a Dart file, what you are going to do is type application and Dart, and then you just have your source, where it is located:

```
<script type="application/Dart"
src="Darttut.Dart">
</script>
```

Make sure you close off the script tag. That is a common error that people make. Because we are going to be converting our Dart files into JavaScript. Mainly Dart is used because the object-oriented part of it is a little bit easier to understand than what we will have with JavaScript. We can basically take advantage of the easier to understand version of Dart, and convert that Dart code into JavaScript.

How do we convert the Dart code? If you are on Windows, go to your command prompt. If you are on Mac or Linux, you are going to go into your terminal, and you are just going to type in after you are done writing all of your code:

```
$ Dart2js -out=Darttut.js Darttut.Dart
```

Hit **Enter** and it is going to convert everything to JavaScript for you. It is very easy to use. That is all we are going to do here, html wise.

Let's start writing some code

Commenting in Dart

First off, if you want to have comments, just put two forward slashes and the word Comment.

```
1    // Comment
```

If you want multiline comments, just do this:

```
2    /*
3    * Multiline
4    */
5    void main () {
6    }
```

Importing Libraries

If you want to import libraries, just write:

```
import 'Dart:html';
```

That is going to allow us to interact with our html document. We are also going to import another math library:

```
import 'Dart:math';
```

That is how we are going to be able to import libraries. The first thing we are going to do here is set it up so the user will be able to go onto the browser, type in two (2) numbers, hit **Add** and then it will show you the calculation, or the math that is involved.

Just to get this out of the way, if you wanted to have a constant inside of Dart, you are going to type in:

```
void main()   {
const double piValue = 3.14;  }
```

This is the way we are going to be able to define a double, or a floating point unit with decimals.

Click Listener

Now what we are going to do is add a Click Listener to the **Add** button, so anytime the button is clicked on, it will execute an application.

To add a Click Listener to the **Add** button, indicate exactly what IDs you are trying to target, and the function you want to execute whenever the button is clicked on:

```
void main() {
    querySelector("#button").onClick.liste
    n(getSum) ;
}
```

A common error is to forget the hash (#) symbol, so make sure you remember to put that in.

Now we are going to create that function. And if this function isn't returning anything, type in void:

```
void getSum(MouseEvent event) {
}
```

It is a mouse event, because that is the way it was triggered.

Casting

Now what we want to do is get the value that was entered in the top and bottom lines of the browser, then add them up, and update the calculation. If you want to get that value, and add it together, you need to create an integer. If you want to perform arithmetic, you need to convert it from a string (which is what num1 is going to be when you get it from the browser) into an integer.

    int num1 = int.parse

This is going to work with all of the different data types, converting from strings to integers.

querySelector

Inside the parentheses is whatever you are going to be targeting. Remember the hash (#) symbol. After that, we'll pull this information from an input element (our examples are meant to be all on one line unless there are blank lines, a change in the level of indent or semi-colons delineating):

```
int num1 =
int.parse((querySelector"#num1") as
InputElement).value);
```

Later on, we will get into all of the different elements that we are going to be able to work with. That is how we can grab that value that is in the input element and bring it over. We are going to do the exact same thing for *num2*.

```
int num2 =
int.parse((querySelector("#num2") as
InputElement).value);
```

You can see little errors come up on the bottom of the screen. That is just saying that we are not using them. Don't worry about that.

If you want to create a variable, and not assign it a type (which basically means you are going to be able to switch from one type to another), we are going to type *var* and whatever the variable name is.

```
var sum = (num1 + num2).toString();
```

Perform that arithmetic and convert it into a string. If you want to put something into your HTML document, it needs to be a string.

Now we need to update calculation with the actual calculation that is going to be performed. We will use **querySelector** again. You are going to use *sum*, so you can get access, and type *text* because we want to change the text.

```
querySelector("#sum").text = "$num1 + $num2 = $sum";
```

This is how we are able to format strings.

Now we are going to jump to the browser and convert that into JavaScript. We will type in 6 in the top line of the browser, and 7 in the bottom line, and hit **Add**. Afterward you should see the following in the browser:

Calculation 6 + 7 = 13
   6
   7

You can see that it updates and puts that little equation up there. So, this is how we'll pull information from our HTML script, update it and do a whole bunch of other things. Now let's go in and take a deeper look at variables.

Variables

To keep this very simple, we are going to call a function, and give it a name *varTest*. All of your execution begins with "**void** main()". Everything starts there and ends there. Of course we can call other functions outside of it *(unlike in some languages functions can be defined below where they are defined)*.

```
void main()  {
varTest() ;
}

void varTest() {
}
```

Then we are going to create this function. It is not going to receive any parameters passed to it. That is why the parentheses are empty.

Dart has 6 variable types: **Integers, Floats, Booleans, Strings, Lists**, and **Maps**. Those are your different data types. We are going to work with all of them.

If you want to create a variable that does not have a defined data type, and just let Dart figure out what the data type is, you just type in *var*. Of course, you can do the same thing with your strings.

```
void varTest(){
void myName = "Jordan";
```

However, we can also specifically define a data type. Let's call it *Random String*. And as you can see, you can do it either way.

```
String randString = "Random String";
```

Booleans are defined with **bool**. They can either hold a value of **true** or **false**.

```
bool canVote = true;
```

You are also going to be able to store integers. The maximum integer size is **9007199254740992**.

```
int maxInt = 9007199254740992;
```

The minimum is going to be the negative version of that. As per doubles, you are going to be able to store pretty large numbers inside of them.

```
double piVal = 3.141592653589793;
```

Just understand that they are only going to have 15 digits of precision. Anything over 15 digits - decimal-wise - is not going to be precise. You can't really rely on it.

Let's do query selector again, and change the output. The portion of the browser underneath the **Add** button has the ID of output.

You are going to be able to put these values between curly brace brackets and perform arithmetic directly inside of there. If you want a new line, just put \n.

```
querySelector("#output").text = "Max Int
: ${maxInt + 1}\nPI : ${piVal +
0.0000000000000001}";
```

If you convert that into our JavaScript, you can then press reload in the browser, and you will see those number add out in the browser. The browser should look like the following (Add = an Add button):

Add
Max Int: 9007199254740992
PI: 3.141592653589793

You are also going to notice that we have this big number on line **15** ending in **992**. Even though we added **0.0000000000000001** to it, it still comes back as ending in **992** in the browser. The same thing happens with the double. So just be aware that you can only have numbers of such a large size.

Let's get rid of that and create Lists. Let's this be a random list. We are going to get more in detail with this later. We will also be able to create Maps, or culminations of key valued pairs. 1 will be the key and "Tom Smith" will be your value.

```
void varTest(){
   List randList = [1,2,3,4] ;
   Map  randMap  =  {1:  "Tom  Smith",  2:
   "Betty"};
}
```

You will notice that you are going to separate your key values with a colon (:), and then separate the different Map items with commas (,). That is how we create all those different data types.

Math

Now let's jump over and take a look at all the different Math functions that are available to us. We are going to call this *mathTest*. One thing that is good to know is if we want to create a random number, just type random = new Random. This will allow us to create random values. We are going to create another one called number = 6.45.

```
void mathTest() {
```

```
var random = new Random();
var number = 6.45;
}
```

The way we actually get random numbers is to use that random object, and if you want a random integer value, you will see that *nextInt* will tell you exactly what you need to know. The code below will generate a random number between 0 and 100.

```
random.nextInt(100)
```

There are tons of little Math functions. They are provided below. We are using **querySelector** to update the output.

```
14   querySelector("#output").text = "5.0 + 4.0 = ${5.0 +
4.0}\n5.0 - 4.0 = ${5.0 - 4.0}\n5.0 *    4.0 = ${5.0 * 4.0}\n5.0 /
4.0 = ${5.0 / 4.0}\n5.0 % 4.0 = ${5.0 % 4.0}\ne^3 =
${exp(3)}\nlog(1000)       =       ${log(1000)}\nmax(10,5)       =
${max(10,5)}\nmin(10,5)       =       ${min(10,5)}\n10^5       =
${pow(10,5)}\nsqrt(81)       =       ${sqrt(81)}\nround(6.45)       =
${number.round()}\nRandom              Numbers              :
${random.nextInt(100)},              ${random.nextInt(100)},
${random.nextInt(100)}\n";
```

You can see how we are able to perform addition directly inside the table above. You can perform addition, subtraction, multiplication and division, as well as modulus, which will return the remainder after the division.

You can also see all of the different functions: **Log** functions, **max** functions, **min** functions, power functions, and rounding. Also notice that we are using the random number generator to generate a bunch of numbers between 0 and 100.

If you bounce over to the browser and reload it, you can see the results of all those different calculations, including the random numbers:

Add
5.0 + 4.0 = 9
5.0 – 4.0 = 1
5.0 * 4.0 = 20
5.0 / 4.0 = 1.25
5.0 % 4.0 = 1
e^3 = 20.085536923187668
log(1000) = 6.907755278982137
max(10.5) = 10
min(10.5) = 5
10^5 = 100000
sqrt(81) = 9
round(6.45) = 6
Random Numbers: 13, 54, 85

I will leave it to you to play around with those functions, but that is just a basic run down on the functions that are available to you. Of course there is a whole bunch of other math functions we can play around with.

Other math functions: **acos, asin, atan, atan2, cos, sin, tan**

There are also a number of shortcuts that will be available to you. Let's say you had a value x that you wanted to increase by 2:

```
x = x + 2
```

You can shortcut that by typing:

```
x += 2;
```

You have the same thing for subtraction, multiplication, and division.

Shortcuts: +=, -=, *=, /=

Conditionals

Now let's take a look at conditionals:

```
void condTest(){
// Relational Operators : ==, !=, >, <, >=, <=
// Logical Operators : &&, ||, !

  String output = "";

  var age = 13;

  if((age >= 5) && (age <= 6)){
    output = "Go to Kindergarten\n";
  } else if (age > 18){
    output = "Go to College\n";
  } else {
    output = "Go to Grade ${age - 5}\n";
  }

  output += "!(true) = ${!(true)}\n";
  output += "true || false = ${(true || false)}\n";
```

If/Else

We are going to change line 6 to *condTest*, and change the Math on line 10 to *condTest* as well.

```
 4 void main() {
 5
 6    condTest();
 7
 8 }
 9
10 void condTest(){
11    |
12
13 }
```

```dart
void main() {
    condTest();
}

void condTest(){

}
```

Below are the various relational operators that we're familiar with:

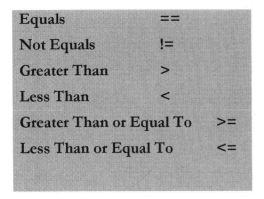

Equals	==
Not Equals	!=
Greater Than	>
Less Than	<
Greater Than or Equal To	>=
Less Than or Equal To	<=

You are also going to have logical operators.

And	&&
Or	||
Not	!

Let's go in and use some of these. We are going to create a string and call this output. We are going to use this to make it easier to output information into our browser.

Let's also create an age equal to 13. We are letting it automatically create that. For an *If* statement, we can say something like *if age is greater than or equal to 5 AND age is less than or equal to 6*. Then we will use brackets and change output to "Go to Kindergarten."

```
void condTest() {
   String output = "";
   var = 13;

   if((age  >= 5) && (age <= 6)){
   output = "Go to Kindergarten";
   }
}
```

Make sure that your code is closed off. Let's throw in another condition. To do that, we will just say *else if* and use another condition like age is greater than 18.

```
output = "Go to Kindergarten";
} else if (age > 18){
```

We will change the output to "Go to College" and add a new line. Finally we will say *else* if none of the other things match. We will want to change our output to "Go to Grade" in quotes, use a dollar sign, and then we will perform a little arithmetic with age minus 5, and throw in a new line:

```
output = "Go to college\n";
} else {
output = "Go to Grade ${age - 5}\n";
}
```

We can do other things with these different relational and logical operators. We are going to get our output again, and see what happens when we put the *not* symbol before the true. Similarly, we can see what happens with the *or* symbol:

```
output += "!(true) = ${!(true)}\n";
output += "true || false = ${(true ||
false)}\n";
```

Switch

Now let's take a look at Switch, and how it works. First we are going to create a string:

```
String superhero = "Superman";
```

The *switch* statement is going to be used whenever we have a limited number of things we want to check for. We will type in *switch* and whatever the variable we are going to be working with inside the parentheses.

Then we are going to check whether the value for superhero is equal to "Batman." If it is, we will change the value for output. We will say something like, "Batman is Bruce Wayne."

```
switch(superhero){
case "Batman":
output += "Batman is Bruce Wayne\n";
break;
```

If we do not want to continue checking all of the different things, which most of the times we do not want to, we'll put a break there.

Then we will do another condition by saying *case*, then the value for superhero, which is what we are checking against. If that is equal to Superman, we are going to do the same thing, then break out of that.

```
case "Superman":
output += "Superman is Clark Kent\n";
break
```

Then the default, if nothing else, comes back as true, we are going to have our output as "Hero isn't in database" to close it out:

```
default:
output += "Hero isn't in database\n";
```

Finally after all of that is done, we will use our **querySelector**, which will allow us to update our output id that we have. Then just reference the text, change it, and throw output into that.

```
}
querySelector("#output").text = output;
}
```

Then we are going to convert it into JavaScript and reload the browser. You should see this in the browser:

Go to Grade 8
!(true) = false
true || false = true
Superman is Clark Kent

So, "Go to Grade 8" is what was calculated. When we use *not* (!), it will convert whatever is inside of the parentheses (**true**) to its opposite (**false**). If either **true** or **false** is true, it will come back as **true**. "Superman is Clark Kent" came back as a match with the switch.

Looping

Now let's take a look at how Looping works within Dart.

While

```
2  import 'dart:math';
3
4  void main() {
5
6    loopTest();
7
8  }
9
10 void loopTest(){
11   String output = "";
12
13   int i = 0;
14
15   while(i <= 10){
16     output += "$i, ";
17     i++;
18   }
19
20   output += "\n";
21
22   querySelector("#output").text = output;
23
24 }
```

Change line 6 to *loopTest*, as well as the *condTest* on line 10.

```
6     loopTest();
7
8     }
9
10    void loopTest() {
```

Then we are going to create an integer called (i). A while loop is going to look very similar to what you are used to. We'll put our first condition. While that condition is true, we are going to continue to perform different calculations over and over again.

```
int i = 0
```

We will put a dollar sign ($) and (i). Since we are not performing any other calculations, we can use the curly brackets (Some people do). We can use the shortcut for incrementing, which is exactly the same as if you were to say (i + 1). Those two things are equivalent.

```
while (i <= 10){
output += "$i, ";
i++;
}
output += "\n";
querySelector("#output").text = output;
}
```

Then we can come in and do our output again, plus or equal to, then throw a new line into it after it is all done. That is the simple way that we are able to use while loop. Not much different from most programming languages.

Do While

We are also going to have the option to use Do While loops, which is what you are going to use if you want to guarantee you go through your loop at least one time.

Here we are also going to throw in a value for (i). Here you actually decrement this. So, you can actually use that (- -) shortcut as well.

```
do {
output += "$i, ";
i--;
}while(I >0);

querySelector(#output").text = output;
}
```

We will also put our while loop at the end of it, indicating we want to continue performing that decrement on that value, as long as (i is greater than 0). Don't forget the semi-colon (;) at the end.

And that is how **Do Whiles** work.

For Loop

We are also going to have For Loops. A For loop is used so that we can have everything self-contained into our loop structure, and that we won't have the decrementing values. We do not have to worry about what is outside of the loop.

For example, we can create a variable of (j), giving it a value of 1. In this example, we'll say that we want to continue looping until (j) is less than or equal to 30. We'll say that we want to increment that. We do not put a semi-colon (;) there.

```
for(int j = 1; j <= 30; j++){
```

Continue

Inside the For loop, we are going to demonstrate how Continue works. We can take j and modulus of 4. Basically what we are saying is if j is a multiple of 4, we want to do something. The thing we want to do is continue.

Continue means, skip everything that follows the rest of our loop and just jump up the top of the For loop, increment the value of j, and continue on. So that is what Continue does.

```
if((j % 4) == 0){
continue;
}
```

Break

Now let's perform another condition, if j is equal to 25. We can say that we want to break out of the loop. This means end the loop execution. That is what break does.

```
if(j == 25){
break;
}
```

Otherwise, we could say *if j modulus 2 equal to 0*, which means it is a multiple of 2, or an even number. Then we want to change our output. So we copy the output and paste it in after the Do While loop. Then let's also paste it in after our For loop is all done.

Let's create one more here so that we have a little more information. We can also create a multiplication table. We are going to say **k** is equal to **0**, then continue looping until **k** is less than or equal to **10**, and increment the value of k each time.

Then let's throw another for loop inside of it. This one is going to be l is equal to **0**, and we will continue looping as long as l is less than or equal to **10**. Then we are going to increment l. Then we can have our output, change the value of that, then get the value of **k** times the value of l is equal to, and then perform our little calculation and a new line.

```
output += "\n";
if(j == 25){
break
}
if((j % 2) == 0){
  output += "${j}, ";
  }
  }
  output += "\n";
for(int k = 0; k <= 10; k++){
  for(int l = 0; l <= 10; l++){
  output += "${k} * ${l} = ${k*l}\n";
```

```
    }
  }
  querySelector("#output").text = output;
}
```

If you reload the browser, you can see all of the different calculations we did. Our While loop is going to be printing from 0 to 10. Our Do While loop, which is going to be decrementing, so it will go from 11 to 1. Then we have our For loop, which is going to print out all of our even numbers.

However if it is a multiple of 4, we are not going to print it out. As you can see, none of the multiples of 4 printed out. Even though this was supposed to go from 1 to 30, it will go from 1 to 25, because of the **j <= 10** portion of our code. We can also see all of our multiplication tables.

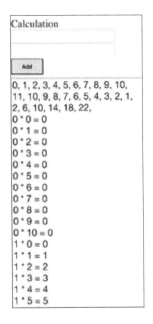

So there was the rundown on looping. Now let's take a closer look at strings.

Strings

Strings will be created whenever you surround something with double quotes ("), or single quotes ('). Most of the time you are going to be using double quotes. If you want to concatenate, or combine strings, type:

```
void stringTest(){
String output = " ";
String randString = "I " + "am a long " +
"string";
```

We can create another one, so we can work with the two of them:

String randString2 = "Other random string";

Now we can get the output. Let's say the 0 index, or the first index. To get the value that is stored inside of there, or the very first element in our string, we are going to type in the string's name and, 0 and place curly brackets { } around.

```
output += "0 Index: ${randString[0]}\n";
```

We can also come in and compare these different values by typing *Strings equal*. Then we can see if they are equal to each other. We can put strings equal with *randString.compareTo*, and the string you want to compare it to, and then close that off with a new line.

```
output += "Strings equal
${randString.compareTo(randString2)}\n";
```

That is how we can compare strings, not with equal sign, but with *compareTo*.

We can also check if a string contains a certain word:

```
output += "Word long in string :
${randString.contains("long", 0)}\n";
```

Long is going to be the word we are looking for. Then afterwards we indicate what index we want to start searching from. We will start from the very first one. You don't need to use that. You can start searching from another index if you like.

We can also get the index of a match. *Long* is what we want:

```
output += "Index of long :
${randString.indexOf("long")}\n";
```

We can also replace. Rather than output this information, we can save it to another variable. Here we are going to say that we want to replace all of our spaces with a comma (,) and a space, then close off with a curly bracket (}).

```
output += "Replace spaces :
${randString.replaceAll(" ", ", ")}\n";
```

We can also split our string into a list. We have to tell it how we want it to split. Here we are going to split all of the words based off of spaces between the words.

```
List listWords = randString.split(" ");
```

We are also going to be able to get the length of a string.

```
output += "String Length :
${randString.length}\n";
```

We can also get a substring from inside. For example, let's start at the very first index, going to 4 spaces in. Here we want to get the first four characters of our string.

```
output += "Index 0 - 4 : ${randString.substring(0,4)}\n";
```

You can see there are many different ways we can work with strings. We can also change the string to upper case with a simple function.

```
output += "Uppercase :
${randString.toUpperCase()}\n";
```

Likewise, we can also convert a string to lower case.

```
output += "Lowercase :
${randString.toLowerCase()}\n";
```

We do this because it might make it easier to search for words if we know everything is upper case or lower case.

We can also trim our strings, which means we just get rid of any leading or trailing white space. We can save it back into random string afterwards if we decide we don't care about the original version.

```
randString = randString.trim();
```

We are also able to trim just white space on the left or right. Trim Left is demonstrated below.

```
randString = randString.trimLeft();
```

We are also able to check if a string is empty,

```
randString = randString.trim();
output         +=        "Is        Empty       :
${randString.isEmpty}\n";
querySelector("#output").text = output;
}
```

That is basically all the different things you are going to be using a lot. One error at the bottom is going to say we did not use list words. We will get to cycling through all that stuff in a moment.

Now let's convert this into JavaScript. You can see in the browser that **0** index is **I**. Strings are not equal, so that came back with a value of **-1**. Is the word *long* in string? Yes it is. Index of long starts at the **7**[th] index. We replaced all of the spaces with a comma (,) and a space.

String length is **18**. It grabbed the first four letters. Next line it converted everything to uppercase. Next line converted everything to lower case. Is it empty? No, so it came back as **false**.

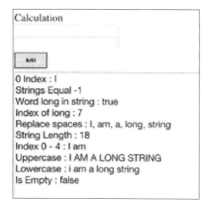

Next let's take a look at functions.

Functions

Let's create a whole bunch of functions:

```
void funcTest () {
String output = "";
```

You can call a function by name and pass in the different parameters you want it to use. Here we are going to perform a multiplication of 3 times 34. Let's call our function *getMult*. At first it is going to create an error saying "you have not created that function yet." That's not a problem. We will create it in a moment.

```
output += "3 * 34 = ${getMult(3,34)}\n";
```

Now let's actually create *getMult*. This is going to return an integer, so put *int* inside. Its name is *getMult*. We are going to define the data type for the different parameters that are passing in.

We expect an integer, and another integer to be passed inside of there. Everything is going to be surrounded with curly brackets {}.

```
querySelector("#output").text = output;
}
int getMult(int num1, int num2){
```

Then we are going to define an integer here.

```
int val = num1 * num2;
```

This is called a Local Variable. It is a variable that is only going to be available inside of this function. If you try to get the value of *val* outside of this function, you are not going to be able to get it. You can play around with that for homework to see how you cannot get the value of *val*, even though it was created in this function:

```
return val; }
```

Then we will just return the value. That is how we are able to call the *getMult* function.

Single Line Functions

You will also be able to define a function on a single line. Let's say we wanted a function that just doubles whatever gets passed into it:

```
times2(num) => num * 2;
```

That is how you would create a single line function. Pretty useful. We are going to call that here:

```
output += "56 * 2 = ${times2(56)}\n";
```

Let's go and create a couple more functions. Let's say we want to add a list of items from 1 to 10.

```
output += addList(1, 10);
```

This is actually going to return a string that is going to be stored directly inside of outputs. It will add a list of items.

Optional Parameters

If you want to make a parameter optional, you need to surround it with brackets. You are still going to define the data type. If you want to give it a default value, you put **=1** inside the brackets. If it is a default value, you do not have to put a value inside of there. I'm just showing you 2 different things instead of 1.

```
String addList(int start, [int quantity = 1]){
```

Now let's go and create a string, which we will call *strList*. The way we are going to calculate this, or create it, is we'll cycle through values using our For loop, while i is less than or equal to the quantity that was or was not passed inside. Remember, it is optional since it is inside the brackets.

```
String strList = "";
for(int i = 1; i <= quantity; i++){
```

We can then get our string list. You can always concatenate

strings, or combine strings by using this shortcut method. We can then separate all of those values with commas (,) and spaces. After we have created our string list, we can return those values.

```
strList += "$i, ";
}
return strList + "\n";
}
```

That is how we are able to use default values as well as parameters that are optional.

Pass Function as Parameter

We can also pass functions just like any other variable. Let's create *times3*, just like we used *times2* above. This will be a single line function.

```
times3(num) => num * 3;
```

That is going to pass whatever values pass inside by 3. Now let's perform a calculation of 67 times 2 is equal to. We are going to create a function below that is called multiply.

It is going to be passed in some number. It doesn't matter what it is. It is also going to be passed in a function that is going to be passed inside.

```
output += "67 * 2 = ${multiply(67,
times2)}\n";
```

Of course, you can do this with any function, not just single line functions. Now let's do pretty much the same exact thing for the other function. We will change 2 to 3, and then we will have *times3* passed inside there.

```
output += "67 * 3 = ${multiply(67,
times3)}\n";
```

Then we will come down and create our multiply function. It is going to return an integer. It is going to get an integer passed inside of it. For the variable after *int num*, you can put anything you want.

You don't have to define what it is. Below we are going to use *func*, but it can be anything. Then to multiply or use that function with the supplied value, just type *func(num)*.

```
int multiply(int num, func){
return func(num);
}
```

It is very streamlined and easy to use. We will execute all of this in a second. One final thing I want to show you is how Recursive Functions work.

Recursive Functions

Recursive Function is a function that calls itself. It sounds way more complicated than it is. Hopefully this one example is going to show you how it works.

Let's say we wanted to get the factorial of 4. We are going to create another function called *Factorial*. Then we are going to pass the value of 4 inside of it.

```
output += "Factorial of 4 =
${factorial(4)}\n";
```

Then we are going to scroll down and create factorial. It is going to return an integer called *factorial*. It is going to receive an integer that we are going to call *num*.

```
int factorial(int num){
if(num <= 1){
```

This next part is very important. Every Recursive Function needs a way out, or a situation which it is not going to be calling the function to execute again. In this situation, once it gets to where the number is less than or equal to 1, it is going to return a value of 1, and stop performing calculations. Else if it isn't, it is going to return *num* times, and then it will call itself again. Here we are going to decrement the value of num.

```
return 1;
} else {
return num * factorial(num - 1);
}
}
```

Let's get all of that saved and reload it. You can see in the browser, all of the different calculations that were being performed. Let's grab the **querySelector** and paste it after the output factorial so we can get all of our results. Then change it into JavaScript and run it.

```
querySelector("#output").text = output;
}
```

Save that into JavaScript and reload it. You should see in the browser all the different calculations that were being performed, from our *getmult* and passed in functions, to our list, that was just a string. You can also see how the factorial was calculated.

It makes sense to go into a little more detail to see exactly how the factorial works. The first time that we cycle through our factorial function, we are going to have a value of 4 passed in. Then times factorial with a value of 3 passed in:

```
1st: num = 4 * factorial(3)
```

The second time we call our factorial function, *num* will be equal to 3. We are going to multiply that times factorial of 2, because we decremented that value:

```
2nd: num = 3 * factorial(2)
```

The third time through *num* is going to be equal to 2 multiply times the factorial 1:

```
3rd: num = 2 * factorial(1)
```

That will kill our function, where we are not going to be calling our factorial function again. The last line is equivalent to 2 times 1, which will be equal to 2.

```
3rd: num = 2 * factorial(1) = 2 * 1 = 2
```

Now let's perform the rest of our factorial calculations, using 2 at the end of the 3rd *num* line:

```
1st: num = 4 * factorial(3) = 4 * 6 = 24
2nd: num = 3 * factorial(2) = 3 * 2 = 6
3rd: num = 2 * factorial(1) = 2 * 1 = 2
```

That is how you perform factorial calculations. We're done with functions. Now let's take a look at Lists.

Lists

Lists are used to store lists of items, which have an index.

```
void main() {
dataTest();
}
void dataTest(){
String output = " ";
```

We are going to call this list *emptyList* because that is what it is. We will also be able to store values inside. We can store multiple different data types inside the list.

```
List emptyList = [];
List randList = ["Jordan", 40, 175.5];
```

We can use For loops to cycle through list items. There is actually a couple of different ways to do this, and we are going to show you them.

One way to do it is to use the length of the list. We can output this as well. Then just cycle through and get all of the indexes. Of course, we also want to convert this into a string because we do not know what they are.

It is very easy to do that even though they have multiple different data types, or could have multiple different data types. Then we can put a comma (,) in between each of those different items, and throw a new line in there as well.

```
for(int i = 0; i < randList.length; i++){
    output += randList[i].toString() + ", ";
    }
output += "\n";
```

That is how you get index values, cycle through them, and print those items out.

For Each

We can also add items to our list just by using the word *add*. Similarly, we can also remove items by using *remove*.

```
randList.add("Pittsburgh");
randList.remove(175.5);
```

We can also cycle through a list using something called *forEach*. What we need to do is put a value inside that is going to hold the list item for us. We also need to define exactly what we want to do with it.

```
randList.forEach((val)  =>  output  +=  "List
Item : ${val}\n");
```

That is how "for each" works.

For In

Another way to cycle through those is with *For In* data type value in rand list, then output whatever the value is, and convert it into a string. Then to the end of that, concatenate with a comma (,) and a space, and paste a new line.

```
for(String val in randList){
    output += val.toString() + ", ";
    }
output +- "\n";
```

So there are 3 different ways you can cycle through list items. We can also define a list that is going to force the user to only be able to hold one type of data. We can type in any different data type, but we are going to use string here.

```
List<String> friends = ["Bob", "Tom"];
querySelector("#output").text = output;
```

You can see how all of this cycles through our For loop and prints out different data types in the browser.

Jordan, 40, 175.5
List Item: Jordan
List Item: 40
List Item: Pittsburgh
Derek, 40, Pittsburgh

We added in Pittsburgh and removed the weight. We called a *For Each*, and used the *For Each* block to print out all of the different list items. We also used the *For In* way of looping through to print out all of the different data types, and the weight 175.5 is now missing.

Maps

Now let's take a look at Maps. A Map stores a key value paired, just like we discussed earlier. It is very important to remember that it is not ordered. Map can hold any data type, but whenever you have your keys, all the keys must be unique.

```
import 'Dart:html';
void main () {
dataTest();
}
void dataTest(){
String output = "";
```

We are going to create an empty Map, just to show you how an empty Map looks like.

```
Map emptyMap = {};
```

Now we can create another one. Let's say we wanted to have one that is state capitals. Remember, you can use any data type that you like, but this is unordered. We are going to separate all of our keys and values with colons (:). We'll use commas (,) for separating the different Map types.

```
Map stateCapitals = {"Alabama" :
"Montgomery", "Alaska" : "Juneau"};
```

There you go. We've just created a Map. We are going to create another one, just to show you we can use different data types. Remember the keys have to be different for all the different types. We can even put multiple Maps inside of Maps. We'll provide name and balance in the same Map.

```
Map customers = {100 : {"name" : "Paul
Smith", "Balance" : 120.25}};
```

Then we can go and output this information on our screen. We are going to get our state capitals by passing in our key, then closing off your entire string.

```
output += "The capital of Alabama is
${stateCapitals["Alabama"]}\n";
```

We will also be able to get our customer information by paying reference to the Map's name, and we can target a specific key (100) and "Balance."

```
output += "Paul Smiths balance is
${customers[100]["Balance"]}\n";
```

We can also come in and change the value of a Map. Here we are going to change 100 and target "Balance" again in this situation. Here Paul came in and paid off his debt. The output will change because of that.

```
customers[100]["Balance"] = 0.00;
output += "Paul Smith's balance is
${customers[100]["Balance"]}\n";
```

We will also be able to remove Map items. Here we are going to remove whatever has the key of *Alaska*.

```
stateCapitals.remove("Alaska");
```

We can also add a new item.

```
stateCapitals.addAll({"Arizona" :
"Phoenix"});
```

That is how we would add an item into our map. You can also use *For loops* or *For each*. We will use *For each* here. If we wanted to get the keys and the values, we just type in both of those different items. We also want to print out the key and the value on our screen.

```
stateCapitals.forEach((k, v) => output +=
"${k} : ${v}\n");
querySelector("#output").text = output;
}
```

Now convert it into JavaScript and run it. You can see it comes back with capital of Alabama as Montgomery. Paul Smith paid off his balance. Alabama, Montgomery, Arizona, and Phoenix printed out in our browser from our For each block.

That is how we work with lists and Maps.

Manipulating HTML

Let's take a look at how we can manipulate HTML. **querySelector** provides us with multiple different actions that we can perform with it. It is also going to allow us to return an element object that can be used to manipulate elements if we provide it with just an id. Here we are going to use calculation, which has an id of sum.

```
import 'Dart:html';
void main() {
manipulareHTML();
}
void manipulateHTML(){
String output = "";
```

We can say we want an Element Object, which we will call *title*. We can use **querySelector**. Since sum is an ID, we are going to use a hash there (#). **querySelector** returns an Element object that can be

used to manipulate the element with the provided ID.

```
Element title = querySelector("#sum");
```

Now we are going to be able to do all kinds of things with it. Easily, we will be able to go and set the value of it.

```
title.setInnerHtml("Take me to your leader");
```

We can also change the color of our element object. We can put a hexadecimal code in there, or we can just use *Blue*.

```
title.style.color = "Blue";
```

You can also define a style, which is the best thing you normally would want to do. This style change is just a font size change.

```
title.classes.add("titleStyle");
```

We are going to output some information as well, to show you how easy it is to get the value that is stored inside that HTML element.

```
output += title.innerHtml + "\n";
querySelector("#output").text = output;
```

If we reload it, we can see "Take me to your leader" in the browser. We've changed the size and the color. It also shows up below the **Add** button because of the output line.

That is how to manipulate elements as well as get information out of them in a couple of different ways. Now let's go and start adding elements inside of elements.

We are again going to get an element object for a div in this situation. Again, we have to use **querySelector** and just reference *divBox*, because that is the *div* we want to work with.

```
Element divBox = querySelector("#divBox");
```

It is very easy to add a div to it. We are going to say that we want to add a div element to it, so we have to define that. I am going to show you all of the other different types of elements you can also add inside of there.

```
DivElement sampDiv = new DivElement();
```

We are going to get into classes and elements here as soon as we are done with this. Right now we are going to change the text for it.

```
sampDiv.text = "I'm a DIV";
```

If we want to add this new *div* inside of the *divBox* that is already there, this next line will add it to the end.

```
divBox.children.add(sampDiv);
```

Let's create a couple more. This is how you create an anchor element:

```
AnchorElement sampAnchor = new AnchorElement();
```

We can also change the text for that.

```
sampAnchor.text = "Google";
```

We can also come in and change attributes for it by using *setAttribute*. Here, we are going to change the *href* attribute for it.

```
sampAnchor.setAttribute("href",
"http://google.com");
```

We can also change text to the end.

```
sampAnchor.appendText("is here");
```

Then we are going to output this information to see what it looks like, and then go and get the value that is stored in *sampAnchor*.

```
output += "href of link
${sampAnchor.getAttribute("href")}\n";
```

That is how we can get attribute values. You can see everything is very condensed that is going to output there. Then of course you are going to need to call the *divBox*, and say you want to go in and put or add our new sample anchor.

```
divBox.children.add(sampAnchor);
```

That is how we would do that. Why don't we also insert a break statement? You can use any of the different tags to input those directly into your HTML document.

```
divBox.children.add(new
Element.tag('br'));
}
```

Let's save that, convert to JavaScript and reload it to see exactly how that looks like. It should say "I'm a DIV" and "Google is here" underneath the browser.

We can also change IDs for elements. Let's say we wanted to change the id for an input element. We want to specifically target id and make that equal to the input element:

```
inputElement.attributes['ID']        =
"inputElement";
divBox.children.add(inputElement);
```

After creating that input element, we can also add a mouse event to it. We are going to use a single line function and call our **querySelector**. We are also going to change the text on it.

```
inputElementChange(MouseEvent event) =>
querySelector("#output").text = output +
"Input Changed\n";
```

Change Listener

Now we will add a Change Listener to this input element.

```
querySelector("#inputElement").onChange.l
isten(inputElementChange);
```

Convert it to JavaScript and reload. You can see we have our input element, and it says "take me to your leader."

When you type anything in the box below the input element, the input element will show up as changed. It will also print information about google.com

We used many different elements that are available to us. We created anchor elements and *div* elements. Below is pretty much a complete list for you to play around with. The complete list can be found at the link provided at the bottom of the list.

```
// Other Elements : AreaElement, BRElement,
ButtomElement,
// ButtonInputElement, CheckboxInputElement,
ContentElement,
// DListElement, DetailsElement, DialogElement,
EmailInputElement,
// EmbedElement, FileUploadInputElement, FormElement,
HeadingElement,
// ImageElement, InputElement, LIElement, LabelElement,
LinkElement,
```

```
// MapElement, MediaElement, MenuElement,
MenuItemElement,
// OListElement, OptionElement, ParagraphElement,
ParamElement,
// PreElement, RadioButtonInputElement,
ResetButtonInputElement,
// SpanElement, SubmitButtonInputElement, TableElement,
// TextAreaElement, TitleElement, UListElement,
VideoElement
// https://api.Dartlang.org/apidocs/channels/be/Dartdoc-
viewer/Dart:html
```

Classes

Now let's see what we can do with classes and objects in Dart. Just like all other programming languages, your classes are going to define the attributes and capabilities of real world objects. Let's create a class. Remember, this should be outside of all the other different functions. That is very important.

```
import 'Dart:html';
void main() {
oopTest();
}
void oopTest(){
String output = "";
querySelector("#output").test = output;
}
```

Let's call it *Animal*. Our *Animal* class is going to have a couple of attributes. It will have a default of "No Name" for its name. It will also have a sound.

We are going to give this "No Sound." A variable that starts with an underscore (_) will be private and cannot be accessed by code outside of your program.

```
class Animal {
String name = "No Name";
String sound = "No Sound";
int _weight = 0;
```

Getters / Setters

You can define how the user will be able to get that value by typing get weight, then providing that weight. That is a way of hiding those values.

```
int get weight => _weight;
```

We can also define set. If they try to assign a value of weight less than 0, we are going to assign a value of 0, because an animal cannot have 0 weight.

```
set weight(int w) {
```

Otherwise, we are going to allow them to set the weight.

```
if(w <= 0){
weight = 0;
} else {
weight = w;
}
}
```

That is a way to protect our data, and that's how setters and getters work in Dart.

Likewise, we are also going to have Constructors, which are also going to be called anytime a new object of animal type is created. You define that with the *Animal* name, same as the class. We are going to increment the total number of *Animals* we have.

```dart
Animal(){numberOfAnimals++;}
```

We will have more on constructors later. For now let's get into Static Fields and Methods.

Static Fields / Methods

Number of *Animals* in this situation is going to be a static variable, which means it is going to be shared by every other animal object that has ever been created.

Every animal object is going to have the same value. This is how you define something as static. Since we do not have any in the beginning, we are going to assign the integer to 0.

```dart
static int numberOfAnimals = 0;
```

We use the static name again. This is going to return a string. It is not going to receive anything. It will return whatever the current number of *Animals* is. We will convert this into a string, however.

```dart
static String getNumberOfAnimals(){
return numberOfAnimals.toString(); }
```

That is how static variables and static methods work. Basically you are going to use static variables anytime it doesn't make sense for an object to have that value. No *Animal* object would know how many animals were created, so that makes sense for that to be a static variable.

Let's go and create a method for this as well. We are going to have this return some information about our animals. That information will be name, sound, and weight.

```dart
String info(){
return "$name, $sound, $weight";
}
}
```

Constructors

Let's now talk about Constructors. Constructors are a little bit weird in Dart. Methods cannot have the same name, so if you have multiple constructors, you must use what are called Named Constructors.

If you have a situation in which you want to be able to accept all 3 of the different attributes for our object, we will type in *Animal* and whatever you want the Named Constructor to be. We are going to call ours *three* in this situation. We are also going to get weight inside of there.

```
Animal.three(String name, String sound,
int weight){
```

If you want to reference an object's actual value, you use *this*, which will allow you to reference an object, even though you do not know what the object's name might be.

```
this.name = name;
this.sound = sound;
this._weight = weight;
```

We can also come in and use the *numberOfAnimals* and increment that as well, each time a new animal is created.

```
numberOfAnimals++;
}
```

Another thing we can do is create another method. This is going to return a string. We are going to reference *this.name*, and that is how we are able to get a value out of that.

```
String run(){
return "${this.name} runs";
}
```

Now that we created all of these different objects and methods, let's jump up a bit and create ourselves some objects. We are going to create an animal object called *bear*.

```
Animal bear = new Animal();
```

Then we can come in and define some values to *bear*.

```
bear.name = "Buddy";
bear.sound = "Grrrr";
bear._weight = 600;
```

Now we will be able to output all of this information. Then we can reference exactly what we want to pull in.

```
output += "${bear.name} said
${bear.sound} and weighs
${bear.weight}lbs\n";
output += "${bear.run()}\n";
```

We are now able to call the Named Constructor. Let's create a new animal called *tiger*, and name him Saber.

```
Animal tiger = new Animal.three("Saber",
"Rowr", 550);
```

We will be able to output all of that information, just as we did before.

```
querySelector("#output").text = output;
output += "${tiger.name} said
${tiger.sound} and weighs
${tiger.weight}lbs\n";
```

Your objects are not going to access your static methods or fields. If you want to be able to access those, you have to use the class name.

```
output += "Number of Animals :
${Animal.getNumberOfAnimals()}\n";
```

We can save that, and if we reload it, we'll see:

Buddy said Grrrr and weighs 600 lbs
Buddy runs
Saber said Rowr and weighs 550 lbs
Number of Animals: 2

That is how we work with or create those objects.

Inheritance

Now let's take a look at Inheritance. We are going to be inheriting from a class, which means we just want all of the attributes and methods that are inside of that class. Let's say we want to create a new class called *Dog*.

```
class Dog extends Animal{
```

That's all you need to do. Now you have access to all those methods and everything that was created in the Animal. We can also create or extend this by saying our dog Animals are all going to bite.

```
String bite(){
return "${this.name} bit you";
}
```

You don't need to go in and create the name. It is already there. One thing you do have to do though is define all of your constructors. That is something, a little bit different from other programming languages:

```
Dog(){Animal.numberOfAnimals++;}
```

And increment that. We are referencing the *Animal* class here, not the *Dog* class. Likewise, we are also going to come in here and use the Named Constructor for the situation in which we'll pass three attributes.

Again, we are going to do the exact same thing we did with *this* earlier. That is one of the weird things about Dart that is completely different from most programming languages.

```
Dog.three(String name, String sound, int
weight){
this.name = name;
this.sound = sound;
this._weight - weight;
Animal.numberOfAnimals++;
}
```

If you want to override a method, you just type the method in again.

```
String info(){
return :$name, $sound, $weight";
}
```

We can do something like just listing this out.

Super

Now I'm going to show you how we can call the Super version of information.

```
return super.info() + " and bites ";
}
}
```

This will call the colossus version of info. We have also added "and bites."

Let's jump up a little bit and use our inherited *Dog* object. Use the Named Constructor here.

```
Dog rover = new Dog.three("Rover", "Woof", 85);
```

We are going to be able to output this in the exact same way.

```
output += "${rover.name} said ${rover.sound}
and weighs ${rover.weight}lbs\n";
```

We are also going to use the override method.

```
output += rover.info() + "\n";
```

You can see in the browser, "Rover says woof, weighs 85 lbs., and bites." That is how inheritance works.

Abstract Class

Now let's take a look at Abstract Classes. An abstract class can be inherited, however you cannot instantiate or create an object from it. Let's create an abstract class and call it *Shape*.

```
abstract class Shape{
```

Now we are going to create the function that everybody that inherits from the *Shape* abstract class has to implement. It's like a contract.

```
double get area;
}
```

Basically it is saying if you inherit from the *Shape* abstract class, you are going to have to create an area method. Now what we will do is create another class. We will call it *Rectangle*. We'll have it extend the *Shape* abstract class. This is going to have a height and a weight. We can define both of those on one line.

```
class Rectangle extends Shape{
double height, weight;
```

Let's go and use a shortcut way of creating its instructor that you can use.

```
Rectangle(this .height, this .weight);
```

Then what we'll have to do is define our *Area* method. Let's just do this on one line because it is very simple.

```
double get area => height * weight;
```

That is how we can implement that. Now let's create a *Circle* class as well. It is only going to have a radius. But it will implement the *Area* method. **PI** is built-in as long as you have the built-in Math library.

```
class Circle extends Shape{
double radius;
```

Now what we are going to do is take **PI** multiply it by radius times radius.

```
double get area => PI * (radius * radius)
}
```

Now that we have it implemented, we will move up and actually use this abstract class. We have *Rectangle*. We will pass in 5.0.1 and 10.0 values:

```
Rectangle rect = new Rectangle(5.0.1, 10.0)
```

Then let's create a *Circle* class as well. We will pass in a radius of 5.0 value:

```
Circle circle = new Circle(5.0);
```

Now we will be able to output all of that information. We are going to do it the same way as before.

output += "Rectangle Area : ${rect.area}\nCircle Area : ${circle.area}\n";

Another thing that is important is that you can actually instantiate using a *Super Class,* and then cast to a *Sub Class.* We will cast with *rect2* as rectangle, and then call the area on it.

```
Shape rect2 = new Rectangle(5.0, 25.0);
output += "Rect2 Area ${(rect2 as
Rectangle).area}\n";
```

That will allow us to use the *Shape* super class in reference to the subclasses of it. This will give an error because we haven't created the *Circle* constructor at the bottom.

```
Circle(this.radius);
```

If we reload it, you can see Rectangle area and the Circle area will come out as well as the other Rectangle.

Interface

Now let's talk about Interfaces. Whenever you use interfaces, you are going to allow your classes to inherit from multiple different classes.

So, let's create a couple of interfaces. Let's say it has a function inside that when called, says "flies."

```
class Flyable{
String fly(){ return "flies"; }
}
```

We are going to create another one. In this situation it is going to return "bullet bounces off."

```
class Bulletproof {
String    hitByBullet(){    return    "bullet
bounces off"; }
}
```

Now that we have those all set up, we can create another class called *Superhero*. We are going to use "implements", *Flyable* as well as *Bulletproof.* You'll be able to use both of them:

```
class Superhero implements Flyable, Bulletproof{
```

Then we can have String flying description equal to "flies."

```
String flyingDesc = "flies";
```

Then we can have a bulletproof description that say, "bullet bounces off."

```
String bulletproofDesc = "bullet bounces off";
```

Then we have to define the functions that we want to have inside of here:

```
String fly(){ return this.flyingDesc; }
String hitByBullet(){ return
this.bulletproofDesc; }
}
```

Now we will be able to jump up inside of Main and work with it. Let's go and create a *Superhero* object, passing nothing inside of it.

```
Superhero superman = new Superhero();
```

Here we are going to change the flying description of superman:

```
superman.flyingDesc = "flies faster than
a speeding bullet";
```

We are also going to change the bulletproof description:

```
superman.bulletproofDesc    =    "bullets
bounce off";
```

Then we can output this information:

```
output += "Superman ${superman.fly()}\n";
```

Reload it and you are going to see that "Superman flies faster than a speeding bullet."

Mixins

Now let's take a look at **Mixins**. Classes that inherit a Mixin don't have to override methods, but instead, they are used to extend another class. For example, let's say we had vehicles, like a class named vehicle. And let's say that it defines the number of wheels as equal to 4.

```
class Vehicle {
int wheels = 4;
}
```

Let's say that each one of your vehicles you would like to have an ID for them. This is where Mixin would come in. What this is going to do is to make a unique ID for every single vehicle class that you have. We are going to create a unique ID off of *DateTime*:

```
class IdMaker {
int get id => new
DateTime.now().millisecondsSinceEpoch;
}
```

This is a nice way to generate a unique ID off of milliseconds, so it should be pretty unique.

```
class Vehicle {
int wheels = 4
}
```

That is what this does. The *IdMaker* generates a unique ID for all of our vehicles. Now we can say:

```
class Car extends Vehicle with IdMaker{
```

The *IdMaker* is going to generate those IDs. Inside of this we can have:

```
String name = "No Name";
```

Then Car is going to be passed in:

```
Car(String name){
this.name = name;}
}
```

The ID is automatically going to be made for us since we called *IdMaker*. Let's go up and take a look at it. We're going to go back up inside of Main method, and create a car type:

```
Car fordTruck = new Car("Ford Truck");
```

Now what we can do is we can type:

```
output += "Ford Truck has the ID :
${fordTruck.id}\n";
querySelector("#output").text = output;
```

It will get the ID that was automatically generated for it. You can see that the browser now displays Ford truck's ID. **Mixins** are a really awesome way to add some functionality to our class.

Operator Overloading

Now let's take a look at how we can use Operator Overloading. Let's say you have a class and it is named Point, like x, y point. You want it to have x and y points stored inside the class. You want to have a constructor for it as well. We are going to use a shortcut.

```
void overloadingTest(0{
String output = "";
querySelector(#"output").test = output;
}

class Point {
int x, y;
point(this.x, this.y);
```

Let's say we wanted to use Operator Overloading to be able to compare these. You'll need a point sent to this point whenever you are comparing one point object to another.

You are going to say that this will be true when the object's version of x is equal to the point that was passed inside the class. Also when y is going to be equal to point y value, you would type:

```
operator == (Point p) => this.x == p.x &&
this.y == p.y;
```

That is how simple it is to override that operator. Also, we would be able to come in here and show how to override the addition of points. We want to create a new point in which we add values together.

```
operator + (Point p) => new Point(this.x
+ p.x, this.y + p.y);
}
```

You can also override subtraction, multiplication and all of those other different things as well. Now we will create a new two new points called p1 and p2.

```
Point p1 = new Point(10, 50);
Point p2 = new Point(5, 40);
```

Let's see, if the points are equal.

```
output += "Are Points Equal : ${p1 == p2}\n";
```

We can also create another point, and we will call it *p3*. Its values are going to be equal to *p1* plus *p2*.

```
Point p3 = p1 + p2;
```

Now, let's get the values for that:

```
output += "P3 X : ${p3.x} Y : ${p3.y}\n";
```

You can see in the browser, points are not equal. You can also see the values of x, y, and our new point.

Exception Handling

The next thing we are going to look at is Exception Handling. Exceptions are going to allow us to catch errors that otherwise would crash our program. We are going to create a function called *divideNums*, and it will receive numbers 1 and 2.

```
void exceptionTest(){
}
void divideNums(int num1, int num2){
String output = "";
```

Inside of here we are going to verify that they are not trying to perform a division by 0. We do this by surrounding everything with a try block. That is going to protect us. We are going to say:

```
try {
if(num2 == 0){
throw new DivideByZeroError("Error");
}
}
```

In an exception test, we will call ***DivideByZero.divideNums***. We will throw 4 and 0 inside of there so that it most definitely does not accept that.

```
void exceptionTest()T
divideNums(4,0);
}
```

Then we will say if it is not zero, we will provide output for it, because we know it is going to be safe:

```
} else {
output += "$num1 / $num2 =
${num1/num2}\n";
} on DivideByZeroError{
```

Now we can provide different output, or different information regarding the error.

```
output += "Can't Divide by Zero\n";
}
}
querySelector("#output").text = output;
}
```

Now let's define our exception down here. We do that by coding:

```
class DivideByZeroError implements
Exception {
String cause = "Can't Divide by Zero";
DivideByZeroError(this.cause);
}
```

That is how we create a custom exception and how we throw it in all those other things. Up a bit, we will pass Error.

```
} on DivideByZeroError("Error");
```

If we run that you can see "Can't Divide by Zero" pops up in the browser.

There you go! There is a ton of information to get you started with Dart Scripting but, as always, we hope that this has truly been...

Dart Scripting Made Stupid Simple!

FREE GIFT – Dart Code in COLOR

The Code Used in This Volume IN COLOR

Courtesy of our friend Derek Banas (from *New Think Tank*) we are happy to send you a PDF of the code from this volume.

It is even more awesome than it sounds… but in addition this will put you on our exclusive list of **Made Stupid Simple** fans and we will let you know about future titles in the **Made Stupid Simple** Series.

Get your free copy at:

http://sixfigureteen.com/dart

ABOUT THE AUTHOR

Jordan Kaufman has almost two decades of experience in technology centered primarily around enterprise software, audio engineering, and alternative animation techniques.

Kaufman also recently started an online community called www.SixFigureTeen.com which promotes youth entrepreneurship, education and alternatives to college.

He resides in the American Southwest with his amazingly supportive wife and family.

jordanrkaufman@gmail.com
Twitter: @Jordan_RK

Made in the USA
San Bernardino, CA
12 January 2019